REWARD FOR WINTER

Reward for Winter

Di Slaney

Valley Press

First published in 2016 by Valley Press
Woodend, The Crescent, Scarborough, YO11 2PW
www.valleypressuk.com

First edition, first printing (February 2016)

ISBN 978-1-908853-63-9
Cat. no. VP0080

A CIP record for this book is available from the British Library.

Printed and bound in the EU by Pulsio, Paris.

www.valleypressuk.com/authors/dislaney

Supported using public funding by
ARTS COUNCIL
ENGLAND

Contents

PART THREE: BILDR'S THORP

For Alan, with love,
and to Manor Farm House, with gratitude

PART ONE

How to Knit a Sheep

Rehomer's prayer

Bring me the wobbly, the scabby, the beaten,
the oldies, the lost, the could-have-been-eaten,
the wayward, the strays, the nightmares to tame,
the cringers, the timid, the ones with no name,
the mangy, the lousy, the missing-one-leg,
the dirty, the stinky, the too-tired-to-beg,
the crooked, the toothless, the eartorn, the humped,
the knobbly, the limping, the recently-dumped,
the feral, the fearful, the head- and hand-shy,
the last gasp no-hopers, the ones who might die,
the three-homes-already, the stubborn returners,
the deafened, the sightless, the never-will-learners,
the tucked-in-the-corner, the sodden in pee,
bring me all these ones – please, bring them to me.

Aubade at Manor Farm

Up at sparrow's crack, there's no glamour.
Four layers, wellies, gloves, even on days
it gives out fair. My vowels hardened when
we moved in, the same way the north wind
clamps my buttocks tight, puckers lipchaps
and sucks my city lilt through snotcrust whorls
where nose used to be. And the ack-ack-ack of
geese stabs my ears, and the argh-argh-argh
of hens twists my empty tubes with echoes.
Even that big baaaaaaaaaaaa which can fall
soft lands heavy on my chest, refluxed in
frigid gasps like last night's supper. Only
a steady huuumpphh hints at romance, hot
breath fogging up my specs, flecks of half-
chewed chaff impossible to shift when dry.

Creation

In the beginning there was a farmhouse without a field, and a woman and a man without children. The man was content but the woman wanted. The old farmhouse knew, it had always known what the people who lived in it wanted, although most wouldn't listen. This woman listened. She heard the house breathe her thirst through its beams, wear her desire into its scuffed flags. She smelled its loss when wind spat ancient soot down the chimney, saw how every spring wildgreen crept a little closer to the back door. So the farmhouse and the woman made a pact, a promise without words. They sealed the bargain with palmpress to wood, flesh on oak. She proved her faith first, reclaimed the land though it wept scars of rubbish when it rained. The woman marked the field with scent and sticks, walked it over and over till she knew the pits and folds like her own body in the dark. The farmhouse waited, humming on a frequency only she could hear. That first winter, with planting done and everything suspended, she doubted the bargain. The cold seemed to freeze out good intentions, make every possible thing one step closer to impossible. But the house still thrummed its constant *yes*, and when spring returned, and new trees perked first buds east to face the pale sun rising, hope fluttered like greedy sparrows on the feeder.

Diptych

Brick by brick

If I could lift it up and
move it, brick by brick,
I'd gladly build it all by hand
again myself, and pick

the best location here,
against these trees, back
to the wood, view facing clear
downhill towards the stack

of small red chimneys huddled
round the church, where it sat
waiting, calm, untroubled,
four hundred years, knowing that

such vigil would pay off, timbers aching
for it, stone hearth breaking.

Buying it back

Fitting that this field
returns, unharmed,
now that the deal is sealed,
to where they farmed

hard living those long days
before, leaving no trace
but bones and stones, their ways
at odds with my mad pace

stuttering slowly to a crawl
along the sloping rocky track,
across the weatherweary wall
with seedlings pointing every crack,

my greedy eyes fill up with green,
buying it back, borrowing a dream.

Bert's pig

I'm still here in this kitchen, in
the corner where the stove would
sigh slow heat to flush old bones.

Every day I watch her chirping
hens and geese, wiping duck eggs
clear of cling and goo, stacking
brown, green, blue with pencilled
dates on spiral stands.

Her fat cats twirl and beg,
nothing like my sleek shadows
flicking in and out of half light.
They're here too, courting scraps,
scrounging soft words.

When she said my name, the one
she called her best goat, the way
she smiled his horns and grinned
his rough thick coat fetched up
such a rush I nearly choked.

The one I miss waits patiently outside,
snout to door crack. He was my champ,
my heart, my big bad lad. Give him an
inch, he'd be through six more of wood
and nails, closer to me than any other.
My son never forgave me that.

Last week she lost her little lamb, blurred
shop-bought butter with her tears. I'm
not immune, but all I see is smooth pearl
hide, eyes bright, tail perked upright as
we led him down the cellar steps, then
red, red, red weeping channels in the dust,
salt flesh hung in gouges in the roof for
fifteen years, untongued.

Doubtful words

She says it's a long love that has no turning.
She says basic rations are health and happiness,
and in case of doubtful words we must trust our
stock of defence bonds, tally the beasts for market
and spread the year's quota of muck over the fields
before Lady Day rent falls due. She says I should
know what it is, that Dad left me this, the papers
browned by his sweat, fingered by hope and
disaster, counting down days till the hay is all
gathered and the land has been mown. Then we lie
fallow, cut off by the dark with nights slamming
like sashes, saving our tallow for Midwinter Eve,
the rut that restocks us, God willing, she says.

Blue

Each Christmas, he'd change the baling twine
that held his trousers up to festive orange, but
this year he left it blue. He couldn't find a clean
or hole-free jumper in the blanket box, so shut

the lid forever on its Nina Ricci dust and wore
instead the logo sweatshirt that she hated,
scrawled in blue. Squinting, he plucked a nose
hair on each day of advent, chalked off and feted

their demise with chocolate Santas bought for
kids carolling to the farm. They bleated their best
Bethlehem, expecting gold, getting blue. Vape
rings hanging in cold air said he'd failed the test,

forgotten those kind crinkles at the corner of her
eyes, flirting like lost periwinkles on woodland
floors. His shut, he saw her eyelids flicker pain,
the cannula breaking blue on the back of her hand.

Saudade

This year, the dark sat heavy on her
shoulders like the velvet shrug she
used to wear to dances. She played
the old songs in the kitchen, canted
words by rote but didn't feel the
comfort, couldn't find the warm.

The shortest came and went.
Who knew that those had been
the best, ones that flew without
blinking, thrust and zest carrying
them through. Hard now to see it
move without them, hear how

it could be, leaving them behind.
She'd been wary what to wish for,
built it to stand up square, taken
herself out when every natural
screamed she should stay in. Once
doubt had gnawed a corner of her

mind, regret drew up a chair to dine.
The wind griped and jittered omens
down the chimney, rain scratched
tapdance consolations on the glass.
Her graveyard neighbours blanked
her from the shadows, and she wept.

Key

No key for this lock, this
brassknobbed blackened
plate, this door behind a
door which once let out but
now lives in. Handle slips
her fist, half turns to give
too soon, an empty twist,
no catch, no forwarding or
back, no leaving, no admitting.
This door behind a door stands
out of time, asks if she is sure,
if she accepts a thing that
shouldn't be but is, will only
open when her grip is tight
and dry, burning to let go.

Five windows and a door

The first stares east, to the sun rising
and the dead. They watch me without
judgement, neighbours outside time.

The second points the north wind
nose on, shines shapes on glass
downhill to the field at sunset.

This third flanks west like a charm,
hens always in sight, green and blue
giving rise to everything new in me.

The fourth has the best view, southern
sunshine tipping the tops of trees in the
roof void but I don't see, never visit.

The fifth hides under, a surprise to feet
above and head ducked down. In here
I feel them all pass, hold their weight.

This last splits my future from their past,
makes me her double, hanging over the
join to replay yesterday's goodbyes.

Memory bag

is heavier than it looks. It isn't mine,
must be returned. Lost acres bulge
against the plastic, trickle dirt tears from
renthole corners, devolve to dust. Every
boundary dot and dash a tenant's defeat,
every bleat and grunt from livestock books
a plea to stall the slaughterman's knife.
And then his wife's will, taut and dark: him
carrying it all, never able to lay it down till earth
closed over him in the family plot next door.

I hear them as I walk the track, hayday laughter from
towering stacks stirring leaves on trees I've planted,
following the line eastward to the moat. Beyond,
lush military furrows mock my hunger, hold me in.

Roses

I've resisted roses all my life, once vowed
to tear out every stubborn stem, but now
find myself sneaking bushes against a wall,
training stems to twine, grow brave and tall
out of a messy cottage garden border.
You would have hated such disorder,
never let your precious blooms stray
outside their boundaries, make disarray
beyond the neatly edged and razored lawn.

You couldn't bear to let the grass grow
more than one day past its mow
due date, wouldn't wait for anyone to
finish before they started work for you.
They all say we're alike, always on the go,
never let things lie. I say it isn't true.

Barn steps

The three of us perched on the old stone
barn steps; him, me and you, him on my knee,
already washed and ready for bed, alone
with the shadows and sun after tea.

Not really alone, the camera was there,
capturing floral pyjama nightwear,
plus dock leaves and barrows reddened with rust,
crumbling fence posts, pockmarked with dust

and bright yellow socks that covered my shins
to stop me from scratching. And so it begins,
our shifting alliance of loving and baiting
each other, sister and brothers, not waiting

and never quite seeing till nearly too late
what Dad saw that night behind the farm gate.

From the landing

She always found a cat somewhere,
if not a barn then snoozing on a sunny bank
behind the farm. So here she is, hair
drain-straight one side, rag curls the other,

framed by a window the same shadow-black
as her sleek friend. Rusting wire squares
designed to fence out livestock back
up to the field, keep her safe. Seen but

not seeing, lost in thoughts that
stroke of fur and tang of milk had
stirred to mind, she maybe sat
there for an hour or more, doing

nearly nothing. I think I moved away
meanwhile. She never saw me stay.

View from her window

after R.S. Thomas

It could have been a painting rather
than a photo; the way the colours of
the hillside softly beckoned her to love
this view the distant way her father
would always love her. The pink blush
of her nightie darkens in the shadows
to a fading purple; evening throws
a hazy pall into the room, dims the flush
of rosy cheeks from bath time, suggests
that this was just a pause to renew
acquaintance, part of his work. Who
would know how this moment's rest
lifted his heart, his draughtsman's eye
to the lens hot with tears, not cool and dry.

The drive to work

gets harder, the cord back to the farm
stretched to breaking down the A614,
my foot easing off as the hill disappears
in the rear view. And now those happy
hens that marked the halfway are gone,
moved to a new place when the house
was sold, their breakout down the field
edge turned to driveway with proper
parking and no holes to poke and forage
through. Those bobbing triangles kept me
going, when they hoiked their skirts as my girls
do, running like hell when their dinner bell
rings. I still look right though I know they're
not there, wish someone else would realise
that a house needs birds to make it home.

Muck and straw

In sludgy Hunters, my nostrils prick at the strong
plain smell of muck and straw, warmed by the sun
and stirred by the stamp of horses. Such a long
time since I sat in that barn, tuned to the thrum
of a litter tanked out on milk sops
and bread, tucked in a bale safe from hoof
or pitchfork. Mother cat would sit aloof,
out of reach, watchful that her babies stopped
fawning on the quiet girl nosefirst in a book.

I'm in my own barn now. My feral children look
before they cross the path of people, hide hard
lessons beneath a hurling spit. Nothing mars
these silent feeding times, deep breathing
sighs and tongue roll chewing, hot flanks heaving.

Careless

And when you did it again, disappeared without notice
because you couldn't be arsed to text or call, addled by
all the night before bottles of Tesco's Finest, larding
it in your toasty bed with duvet over your eyes and
conscience, it was that smell, that smoky dry waft
of urine-soaked straw that told me it would be OK,
that I could do what I'd done before, by myself, again,
that stubborn sweat would pull it round, even though my
fingers itched to crush your careless windpipe, legs twitched
to stomp my dung-caked wellies on your slackjaw, sleeping face.

Smallholding

Every dawn she looks up, sucks on doing words
to break her fast, breathes in the day. So many
to roll around a mouth starved of soil; she grinds
their grit between her teeth, their loam clagging
under her tongue, a raised bed to plant the seedlings
from her mind. Words like *tupping* and *scouring*,
moulting and *docking*, *dagging* and *flagging*. They
make her smile, these hard sounds that taste as
they paint, no place for dainty ears now. *Crutching,*
fettling, suckling; leaching, pleaching, polling. More
than a syllable string, the day's to do list pinned down
sharp, big tasks made small. In the holding, she
learns what no course can teach; the weaning from
loss, tears drenching *knackerman* and *carcass,*
a voice not her own harrowing life to the wind.

Critical paths

Donkey

I follow the edge,
hug the border,
am pressed so soft
that in a half-light
only hooves as
silent and sure as
these can find
their way home.

Goat

I split and cross go
straight then bend
offer the best and
worst of all positions
challenge the bold
and give the weak
the chance to run
to keep their footing
in the dips and hollows
to lead and see who
follows.

Sheep

I am the way
of the many
led by the few,
I am deep
and true, I
curve as I go
so that fast or
slow, I can show
who comes after.

Rat

I slither and slink, duck under and dither, work
my way round the border and work out safe order
before finding the source; I claim this resource.

Chicken

I am invisible, I am divisible, I am the way
of thousands of feet, taptapping beaks,
dust baths in the sun, squawking flap runs,
skirts hitched to waistlines, wings
beating high-fives, eggs rolled in dirt,
girls born to work, dusk ambles home,
their right to roam.

How to knit a sheep

Start with the legs. It helps to
grab a hoof before casting on, or
he might kick you off. Hold the yarn
taut enough to test his strength,
loose enough to feel his flank quiver
as he bunches shanks to stretch the
ply, hoping it will fray. Loop and dip,
add sufficient stitches to keep his
interest, praise his beauty while
you unravel him, tug gently or he'll
slip your noose. Twist and roll, turn
and back again, keep your palm
against his side as you slide the pins
around about, each click a kiss,
each gartered purl a sweet low
riff to make him give it all, slough
that fleece in one soft piece
to flow from fingertips to floor.
Scoop it up and sniff warm oil
rising through his staple, the crop
he gives up now with grace. Keep
your face pressed to his curls,
breathe the heat and wax of him
behind his ears as hands move
faster as you near the end, his chest
bare and cold, your feet hot under
so much weight. Tie the ends off tight
before you let him go, your nose to his
in thanks only eskimos understand.

Reward for Winter

For the first time in her adult life,
she allowed herself to sweat, to leave
dust under her fingernails, to be
imprecise. As spring leached into
summer, heat snaked through pores
and found her chilly core that
hadn't seen daylight or action
in years. No amount of SPF could
block her thaw once it started;
the field licked folds of her mind
with a green velvet tongue.
Every night she inhaled the sky,
tasted clouds and stars, heard
ten million blades of grass sing
for rain. She stroked the dark like
a cat, rubbed against rough wooden
fence posts till warmth spread inside
out, urging her on. And when she came
back to herself, she could smell every
animal she'd touched on her fingers,
their oils and dirt mixed with her own.
She'd never felt so loose, so unfinished

PART TWO

Washing Eggs

Washing eggs

The utility window looks north to the reclaimed slag heap.

Not all of them will make the grade, although her
standard bends for broader flaws than other keepers
would permit. This thin green shell from eldest hen
sails on through; shock rings round dark brown

The wall recess is one foot thick and stifles footcrunched gravel.

glories are stroked like healing scars from boxing
bouts, while calcium bumps on ovaloid ends
are nipple tweaked to see if they'll drop off. Only
pee wees, rhomboids and excess wrinkles aren't

Today wind turbines face an empty west waiting for the lift and spin.

allowed. These go back to feed the flock in scrambles
forked with thanks. Hands busy with eggs and cloth,
while she wipes she ponders short call pancakes
for monthly grandkids, fry ups for paunches

Geese rear up above the wood and v-form to new fields.

eager for the biggest box, the double yolkers.
And wonders if, like eldest hen, she's reaching her
allotted quota; middle aged skin wearing casual dints,
last eggs queuing up inside, pushing to be laid.

Neighbours' tail lights redden the trellis.

Point of lay

Has it all been building to this
point? Everything up to now
a practice go, experimental kiss
not consummated vow?
I tingle low inside, a flush
of heat that won't allow
more hovering on the fringe. I blush,
unsettled, hide my telling face.

The urge to squat and push,
to finally assert my place,
is forcing me to speak. My choice
would never be to press the pace
and conscript others to rejoice,
but what else can I do? I can't ignore my voice.

Shedding feathers

At first I hardly feel that small
light tug and silent fall
that lies, unnoticed, underfoot.

Flutters of disquiet I put
down to cooler days, the change
and end, a new routine. So strange

to lose sharp appetite
that keeps me centred. By night
I'm chilled, bald underneath,

exposed. No sign of sheath
pricks yet to rebuff shame.
I turn away, deny my name,

skin raw and bare for all to see.
So much uncovered, so unlike me.

Hybrid

One tall, controlled and stately,
one compact, quick and round,
me somewhere in the middle. Lately

I'd begun to worry I was bound
to be this neither nor another,
least of both, the worst of each. I sound

the spit of him and scurry like my mother,
ponder, pause and gauge like him then,
convinced, cannon into bother

that comes to seek me out. But when
it's time for shooting trouble, splicing pays
in spades. They won't mess with me again,

not now they've seen the fast and fatal ways
a hurt can be returned. Serve it cold, Dad says.

Predictable

You really thought you'd got me pegged,
could spot a mile off what I'd do.
In your shoes, I'd think the same
but hope I'd spy the smaller clue.
Track records can be wrong, misleading
indication what comes next.
While faces fake an honest reading,
behind the type sits different text.

Now even if you asked me nicely, begged
and pleaded for my vote, I'd be averse.
Hypocrisy only makes things worse.

Besides, I like to hoard surprises – hold
them ready in reserve. No point revealing
all my assets. Transparency can be a curse
and better to be brave, than bold.

Squat

Don't make the daft mistake of being gentle
with me. I can handle much more than you think.
I might be short and dainty but looks are incidental
to performance. You want it rough? I won't blink
or bat a lash if romping is your hot desire.
Just be firm and fair with me, that's all I ask,
and in return you'll land a bird who'll never tire.

Don't hold back – I'm over equal to the task.
If you're not completely happy when we're done,
I'll refund the difference. I'll even smile
the whole way through, make sure it's fun
for both of us. What are you stopping for? Don't rile
me now by asking if I need a break.

I've told you twice – there's nothing I can't take.

Clipping my wings

It felt terrible at first,
unsteady on one side,
clearly marked among the others, nearly cursed

by a tilt I tried
to minimise. The worst
was how I felt inside,

confidence burst,
appetite gone, diminished.
Just when I feared my thirst

quenched and me finished,
they came back for another go,
and I got just what I wished

for – the chance to fly, to really show
what I can do. Now watch me grow.

Blind gut

Well, it's not often I get chance
for five minutes. As for romance,
can't remember, to be honest.
What with everything else, it's best
to keep a clear head, not get distracted
by unnatural urges. Yes, I was attracted
to the wrong sort in the past, but I prefer
to keep the gories to myself – confer
at your peril, I always say. Some
things are better kept private. Although come
days like these, when I'm relaxed and warm,
nattering to someone nice, what's the harm?

Hutch closer dear, let's not broadcast all my sin
to that lot over there. But better out than in.

Crock

Something not right. From the start
I should have known,
stuck to my guns, stayed apart.
So tempting though, not to be alone,
to savour joy, share a groan,
apprenticed in the art
of joint effort. This mart
of smiling thieves has undertone
with bite, spites to the bone,
bleeds me breathless. But my heart
of stolid stuff, grown
too tough to crack or break,
is fine, wised up. Ignores the fake.

Oddity

This one, one of mine? No, I don't
think so. I'm sure I'd recognise it,
if it was. Mine are normally regular,
neat and short – consistent is my
middle name. So this one can't be mine.

See, it's not even even – there's a very
ugly thick bit, right about *here*. Mine are
finer, much less brash, subtle to the touch.
They leave you wanting more.
This one, I'd be surprised if anyone goes
near it. It has nothing of distinction,
nothing to commend it, save the shape.

Did you get to sleep with the big storm last night?
I felt like I'd been shot by that bright flash of light.

Parasites

Hard to say when signs began to
show, perhaps the last new
moon or maybe the one before?
Sorry love, my mind's not what it was. Saw
how pale I looked this morning, gave
me quite a turn, I can tell you. 'Grave
Digger Grey' I think it's called.
Anyhow, when I peered in close, bald
as well as thin stared back – where did
all those extra layers go? Never hid
my fondness for the odd treat or nibble,
never wanted any of those low fat, no quibble
diet fad things, happy to stay round and cheery.
So what happened? Yes, hold on, be with you in a minute,
   dearie.

Gular flutter

Just stay calm, and remember to breathe.
Everything will be fine.

Fine – stay. Will everything. Remember to
just be calm, and breathe.

Breathe calm. Be fine. Remember to just
stay, and will everything.

Everything calm. To just breathe
will be fine. Stay and remember.

Remember to breathe, be fine
and everything will just stay calm.

Calm will be everything. Fine to breathe,
and remember. Just stay.

Stay and breathe. Fine to remember.
Calm will. Be everything just.

Egg bound

I keep my breathing normal, but I can tell
it's stuck. No matter how I hunch or push
to strain it out, there's no quick rush
to spike the pain, no triumph to expel
it this time, not like before. I doubt
he'll see how much it hurts me,
crouched and ruffled on the floor. He
expects such constant churning out,
peak flow without pause. But today
I just can't do it. It might be age
that slows my quota, rage
that blocks my vent. Or I may
need a gentler hand than he can give.
If it breaks inside me now, I won't live.

Pecking order

Before, I was the one in charge,
or at least allowed to think so.
None as fast, as smart, as large

as me, prepared to tackle low
yet aiming high, fixated on the prize.
But now the only thing to show

for glory days and chartless rise
is thumping in my head.
In this new world of slipshod lies

and scrapping over crumbs, I'm dead
if one more bashing comes my way.
I'm grateful just to sleep, be fed,

stay safe to fight another day.
I'll wait. No rush. I plan to have my say.

Grit

Feed them to me slowly, these
small sharp fragments of rough love.
Choose the ones with harder edges,
make sure you take off your kid glove.

I'm not like all those others – I welcome
tough bits stirred in with the smooth.
I've learned the truth is better for me,
there's nothing secret left to prove.

I'll swallow when I think I'm ready,
don't be anxious that I'll duck the chore.
You've no need to hover nearby –
if I want help then I'll call you, like before.

No reason to stay with me, so go and check up on the rest.
I'll sit here till I'm finished, take time to properly digest.

Broody

Look, I have to do this in the dark
where it's quiet, free of all your
brainless interruptions that mark
and mangle every minute. The score

of stupid questions asked today is ten.
I'm getting to the point of no return,
brewing on the brink. Remember when
I said don't bother me in here? Learn

to fend more for yourself? Which bit
of 'leave me' can't you understand?
You've always been a selfish shit,
get it in your dimwit that you're banned,

banished, binned and duly bollocked. Cough
and mutter all you like, as long as you fuck off.

Red and green

You're a mean bunch,
a sucker punch, a cheap lunch.
What made you all so snide and snarky?
I can't be doing with this malarkey
that trickle wastes our time.
Low blots from hot shots are a crime.
You miss the gist of your great gifts
and focus on the gripes, the gaps, the rifts
and subdivisions self-perpetuated.
Get a grip, guys. You're infatuated
with your own obtuse obsessions.
Cut the crap, the spin, the public prepossessions
and just chill out. Raise your gaze, feast your eyes
beyond the phone box. Graze grass. See skies.

Too long with ducks

They chunter I'm a lost cause, and
frankly, I agree. Yes, I could try
harder to fit in, learn all the reasons why
things should go this way not that, sand
down my edges, smooth the path by
faking praise, forget to make a stand
when bottom line gets panned
and scorned – but then, why should I?

My reputation sears me like a brand,
marks me as too driven, unable to comply
with softer shapes and looser thinking. It's my
past mistakes that teach me that the best land
lies along my own horizon, never buy
the greener rented field. I deal my own hand.

Quota

How will I know when I'm done?
When I'm over, finished, spent?
If I realise my course is run,
will killer kindness meant
to raise me squash all hope,
polish me off with pity? Could
I ever learn to do without, to cope
with no more fire, or flurry? Would
I regret those early bursts of light,
worry that the middle phase
of silent graft at midnight
snuffed me out too soon? Did praise
provoke me past a peak I'll not admit?
When will I know it's over? Is this it?

& egg

A small white bird, waiting at the back,
weighing up her options. She might attempt
to wing it, puff out her orange chest, pre-empt
the strike of sharpened beaks, avert attack
from meaner hens of scornful, worn demeanour.
Or she may stay put, hope no one has seen her,
miss out again on corn and worms: stay thin,
keep wondering what to do to be let in.

Now it's lying here, the palest shade
of arctic green, out of place between the
earthy brown and speckled cream. She laid
this one, no doubt that it's hers. When
he comes back to clear the nest, he'll
hold it up, then smile. Subtle, little hen.

PART THREE

Bildr's Thorp

Nottinghamshire Sheet XXIX N.W.
OS Edition of 1920

Ingar's Holt

is nothing now; no
brushwood, ash or elm,
no marker boundary
to the mor, no bolthole
cover for the son, his
father famed for
everything he lacked,
no bracken beds for
village girls too slow
to run, no heathered haze
to gravel pit, no quick
cut on to Cockett Barn,
no pheasant flush or rabbit
tracelines through the mud.
Nothing left now, none of it.

Wycar Leys

is not the same now; no dairy
for the lord, the kiarr long
gone down to the holt, no
byres rousting pigs to troughs
higgled with turnips, no parlour
maids smirking secrets through
the cream, pressing tokens into
curds wheyed down for love, no
farmhands clagged with clay
dragging their Sunday Best home.
Not the same now, in any way.

Labour-in-Vain

is nowhere now; no farm
of dust and stones to ire
the tithemen used to fecund
work, no bricks or slates or tiles
that propped the granary wall
against the turnip house,
no sickly cows whose milk ran
thin and drenched the empty
calf box, no horses lathered
with the toil of dredging
hard small gains. Nowhere
but here now, this hostile soil.

Parson's Pond

is nobody's tryst now; no rector
eking acres to sweat a shilling,
no fishing rights for enclaved
few, no ribald gossip at the pump,
no carpe diem at the open view,
no ginnel out to Stoney Field,
no windbreak there to choke the
gusts that barrel through. Nobody
trysts now, or knows how to.

Bildr's thorp

He ran from the farm like he was learning to slay,
great grandfather's hounds snouting his heels
with low battle howls, an invisible axe twirling
through grass downhill to the ditch. The half-
remembered hearthtale of severed hands
hovered somewhere north, somewhere hard
and cold and red, somewhere near a shore
far from here, when boats were more
important than carts and jewels as big as
skimstones pinned the eyelids of the dead.
Nothing was owned or held, only wanted.
Movement was everything and settlement a
rumour of old age few would see, or wish for.
He ran from the softness of straw and the comfort
of cattle. He ran because his mother called him
darling, kept him closer than the hounds and
tighter than the bindings on his fox fur boots.
And as he ran, something small and fierce burned
through his chest until it burst on his tongue,
sprayed through the story of the morning in
one long eulalia, herald warrior in waiting
for a past buried under this rocky mound, safe
behind the ramparts of his father's steading.

Initially

It was the first thing I saw when we
recced the house – that huge dark beam
inglenooked under pink sandstone blocks
robbed from church walls. Lights off, it was
impressive, brooding, elemental; the last
remnant of open hearth, twisting spit and
ink-charred meats, slim wavering flames
reaching from the taper to caress wood

in indelible embrace. Lights on, it caved,
revealed more to the eye than a hopeful finger
inching along dusty striations could ever
randomly find. Excited, I cooked up warm
imaginings of a father, mother, daughter, son,
roasting hog and chestnuts over open fires,
intense winter days blurring into nights with the
roar and hiss of fat dripping to dirty flagstones.

Initially I guessed at four, maybe five, names.
Right at the top, the deepest marks made by an
iron hand, someone used to gripping hard,
refusing to let go. Lower down, the same suffix
replicated with a lighter touch, either tired or
idle, or a woman. Smaller on the left, spaced in
relief, not a family but lovers – servants
inchoate in lust, passion fuelled by the acrid

reek of flesh rotating in the half light, sweating
its juices in time to theirs. Then upside down, I
realised my mistake. Not family, not lovers. One
imprint IR I R IR IR IR I R IR I R IR I R IR I R
repeating across, under, backward, forward –
intimate scars on oak. IR alone in silence,
rough carving over and over like a stuck needle,
impelled to show the world what mattered most.

Völuspá revisited

Bildr's lament

With the slip of a vowel, my legend was lost – my
curse to be an eternal short-arse, one of many
brothers banded together by stature into the
collective frown of dwarves. Yes, we all had odd
names – it was easy to mistake Bifur for Bofur,
Northri for Suthri, but he wasn't even a dwarf, for
Thor's sake. He was born with a spoon so jewel-
encrusted, he chipped his perfect pearls before he
could walk. Son of the Valfather, he had it all,
him with his arrogant, awe-inspiring A, shading
my insignificant i into an appendixed apologia. If
only they'd realised it was me who sailed the ships,
rode the horse, won the wars, while he loafed at
home with Nanna, golden idles the pair of them.
If that slow-quill Snorri hadn't been so fixed on
bigging up his mistletoe murder, my squat little
life might have made it out of the strophes, might
be rising now in Valhalla, might be remembered.

Transcript

So what do you want to know?

No, never have found it. Father, when they moved in in '38, it belonged to Rufford Estates, he never found anything. It's all pie in the sky. Same set up, village in Yorkshire, suspected same thing – not saying there weren't but we never found it. Don't know anything about it, never seen it.

Now then, this is in the middle room as was?

Never been back since we finished with Jed up there. Previous lived there were named Fox and they farm at Ollerton, under the railway bridge. The family Fox is still there. I knew his dad. The old man was a card, had a cowboy hat on.

That book by the headmaster, what's his name?

Prior to Townsend, it were Burton, about 50 years ago. A light brown paperback, might be in the library. The cupboard was supposed to be upstairs, a shoe cupboard. Supposed to be true that he hid here, then Southwell, then Newark Castle, then shipped back to London. I grew up knowing that.

Rectory Farm was general purpose, they didn't milk.

We used to milk seven by hand, had a bucket with a vacuum pump on top. Carrying milk from the cattle shed next to the moat, that used to be the cow house. Used to take it to Co-op Dairy where Linneys is now. Manager were there with a big hosepipe making vats of milk, boosting it like. I used to go up there as a lad with him, ten gallon a day.

Did you look in the loft for them books?

My mother was a Hutchinson, that's how close-knit a family the village was. My granddad had the garage, the undertaker, the blacksmith, it was so close-knit. My Uncle Bill did the TV repairs when they brought them in in the fifties. We've got years of history here.

Originally we came from Eakring.

There's a lot of us buried in Eakring church. This is my grandmother's will. That's me, sister had a pony. That's the field at the back of the farm. My sister had what was valuable out the house, she didn't want the stuff that was interesting to me.

Anyhow, you can't choose your family.

Big stone trough in the cellar, don't know how that got there – that was Dad's mushroom trough. Never grew any though. He were a tight farmer, squeaked when he walked. In the bit of the house they took down, there were a pantry with more stone troughs for salting beef. The last pig killed up there, Dad had two hams hanging up on hooks for donkey's years. Dad carved it up and it were beautiful, it had been up there 15 year or more.

1941, that's the parish magazine from Southwell Minster.

That's my mother, that's the farm at the back. That's the old walnut tree there. That was me dad back in 1938. That's what was the farm, it surrounded the church. This was taken from the top of the rectory. I haven't been there since Dad died. I got this by accident from the rector, had his rucksack off him and this was inside it. Yes, he's still alive.

Did they find any guns?

There was an orchard at the back, 20 yards from the house, there were a couple of apple trees, I wondered if they found any guns if they excavated it, old guns. They just buried them in them days, no value you see. In that area, there was a lot of stuff buried, 50 years ago. The guns were here, in this garden orchard, pig run and garden orchard. Everything was orchards. Going up the Brail, on the right up the lane, on the right was orchards, everybody grew their own stuff.

Is any of this any use to you?

When he retired, they sold the land to Imperial Tobacco, then they sold it to Eakring Farms. All the maps link to each other. That's the brickworks, that's the railway, that's the reservoir, that's the edge of the pit. When they sunk the pit they went through the river basin, they used to generate power at the pit to feed the village. You can take these, but I'd like them back. You can keep them as long as you like, as long as you remember where they're from, if you get me.

But as regards the tunnel, no, never seen it.

Vivat rex

*On the occasion of His Majesty King Charles I
hiding in a cupboard in our farmhouse*

This box once concealed a king
in flight, his carefully coiffed curls
dusty and collapsed under the lid
pressed tight against his head. Earls

waited in the woods, in case this box
could not contain his majesty, revealed
instead a short pale man of middle years
in bright red garters, black stacked heels

a damned nuisance in this small space,
vanity almost his undoing. But this box
would not be the one to turn him, too well
hinged to creak its secret. Pride swelled

wooden seams to bursting yet held firm
and fast, proof of lasting craft fit for
the king who clamped his breath inside.
Outside rounder, harder heads than his cried

if God be with us, who shall be against us,
sharpened swords and buffed their cannon
ready for the siege that finally saw their liege
unboxed, defrocked, beheaded, dead.

Ex cineribus resurge 1726

Inscribed on Mrs Outram's house, after the fire

When it started, no one noticed
that bright red line creeping from
the lintel of the smithy, the hot shoe
cast too soon to the tumble of straw,

the white hot line sweeping to the
lane then leaping to the Rectory gate,
cast too soon from a jumble of straw
to the log pile heaped for winter at

Mickledale Lane, leaping at the rector's
gate to Mrs Outram's light, dry thatch,
her log pile proudly reaped for winter
to show Will Hodgson she could cope,

the gate to her tight, dry thatch kept
shut to his advances, the widow firm
in showing Hodgson she could cope,
but the red line quickened, despite

the gate being shut, firm gusts of wind
stoking glints to swaying tapers, and
so the red line thickened, in spite of
the wide gap between, uphill progress

stroking sparks to flaring torches, and
then Cow Lane was set on fire, flouting
the wide gap between the barns uphill
of the Pinfold, the heat carried from

Cow Lane firing the alarms, flouting
all conventions of the glebe, panic
in the Pinfold, the heat harrying the
beasts held to the lord's advantage

in convention of the glebe, fear and
all that smoke making them stampede
like the beasts held for the lord, gain
safety on the eminence by St Margaret's,

stampeding through the smoke straight
into each other's arms, indebted for their
safety to the eminence by the church,
where no one noticed when it started.

Their letters

Her letter   *1st May 1610*

is pressed from flour-damp breast to Judas-hand Joanna,
hides in spinster folds to pass the Hall, makes its way first
to lips then nose, Peter eager for the hard-worked scent of
her, his Rose with lush, wide petals and soft sticky buds,
last pinched and tipped on Hollyn Hill St George's Day
past, under the crab apple and in sudden view of big John
Beale, his face a ruddy fluster, his mouth a sour benediction
recocked to testimony after. Her letter brings an intake of
delight, a crotch twitch of sweet slickness full remembered,
invites him to visit her indoors, her husband Nicholas off to
Lincoln at short call, her window open 10 o'clock this night,
and she will take him in.

His letter   *6th May 1610*

travels safe to Bilsthorpe with trusted Thomas, firm downward
strokes on stiff white parchment vowing more than she could
dream, trapped in this loveless for six cold years, her husband
good for canny trade elsewhere except in bed, a man of stolid
hopes and shuttered heart. His letter teases with dotted i's
and double crossed t's, flushes hot tongue thoughts of curls
and thighs until her forehead pounds, leant hard against
the larder door. His letter pleads to risk again, to meet him
outside her house tonight when the moon averts so not to
be complicit in their sin. His letter in its supple roll enfolds
their last two near escapes and tightens them to nothing, her
sweaty fingers toying with the ribbon, willing to believe.

Her husband's statement   *11th July 1610*

is a blackened growl of grudged restraint, a tamping down of
what would be invective if the form had given room, if the
Magister had asked for more than fact, more than witnesses
had proffered as they lined to spew their sordids into village
rumour pots. Her husband's statement tells he found their
letters (the shame), had them followed (the scandal), offered
battle for his name (the honour), turned down money for
his wife (the strumpet), would not countenance divorce (the
defeat). Her husband's statement spikes the good brown
paper with each ink jab, though why the scribe is angered by
dictation lies unrecorded. Her husband never learned to read
or write; guessed instead their letters meant no good, hidden
as they were inside the corn crock, smeared by too much
touching, her round, white body heat, the smell of inner thigh
when she wore them like a trophy beneath her skirts.

Fox and cubs

(1) *Pilosella aurantiaca*

Sure signs of summer, your shy
russet heads slow bobbing on
the grey church wall opposite my
kitchen window. Much darker

orange than in photos, brighter
than all the bouquets weeping
petals on new graves, lighter
than warm August's whistling

adieu. Sometimes you're late –
no fuzzy black tips! – and fear
that mowers and mourners
have seen you off this year

addles my morning tea. Then
back you come, first ones and twos,
runners spreading drifts out to
glow the green with unconditional

cheer. Grafted, you won't stay in my
garden, don't allow yourselves to stray.

(2) 1911 Census

Farmer Fox, what was your story?
Did you have spare time to chew
a little fat, reap a bit of good life,
stand back and enjoy the view?

One hundred years ago, before the War,
what was the stone trough in the cellar for?
Was it Gladys' or Fanny's morning chore
to fetch water up from the well?

How did Miss Schneider fit into your plan?
Was she really here to nurse your two
girl cubs, or to ease a weary man?
Did Ethel mind? Did her brother know

if so, dear hapless Fred, given bed
and board in trade for time served? Did he
and Joe get on, the younger man dead
set on following you in tenure if

boy cubs weren't on the cards? It
must have been hard. But who were
the other five living here, these
throwaway shards with no names?

Friends of yours from Liverpool days?
Strays to help on all the acres
when weather roared from the north
to wither crops and cattle?

Grafted, couldn't they stay on the
holding? Didn't they pay your way?

The man who taught Milton

They say you make your best friends at Cambridge, and he
believed that as much as he believed in God, found
ease in our conversation and some pecks of peace
in this small spot on the hill here
by the church, my house a home none
had ever thought to offer him elsewhere.

Although we were close, his mind wandered elsewhere
at times, those debates with kings and poets that he'd
been famous for circled down the years, found
wormholes of doubt to corrode the peace
of certainty that spawned them. Here,
he unpicked and unravelled himself, left none

of his own arguments unchallenged, none
of us spared. My wife wished him elsewhere
when things got so bad at night that he
slept and walked together – we found
him hard on his knees on his mother's grave, peace
as far from his tears as the Rectory to the Minster. But here

he was safe, and unknown. And he loved it here,
would filch a pitcher from the kitchen maids who'd none
of them dare to tell, and walk the fields till elsewhere
became somewhere again inside his head. Soon he
started to look well on it, lost that Irish pallor and found
a lightness that I'd missed in his voice, the pulpit peace

stealing over me as I listened to him speak, a peace
as soft as goose down, as white as the moon. I kept him here
as long as I could, but those letters were arriving, none
of them left unopened for long. Elsewhere
kept calling him, he said, and God commanded. He
couldn't stay, wouldn't let himself be found

wanting. So that was the last time. They say they found
him on the floor of the chapel, that it would have been peaceful.
We went to Derby to fetch him, to bring him back here
where we could do things properly, none
of us wanting him buried elsewhere,
somewhere we couldn't visit. I think he's

pleased. The church is quiet, its heart beats slow
and at night I see the hare. He found peace here
when there was none for him elsewhere.

Restored

Drawn to the window every night,
I stand and stare at the same view
that people four hundred years ago might
have seen, admired, when things were new.

I stand and stare at the same view.
The dead look back and stare at me –
some were alive when things were new,
now graves in moonlight are all I see.

The dead stare back and look at me.
Breath steams on glass and blurs reflection.
The silvered graves now hard to see,
my mind turns inward, seeks direction.

Breath steams on glass, distorts reflection,
old wooden beams sigh in and out.
My mind turns inward, misdirection,
undermined by grief and doubt.

Dark wooden beams breathe in and out,
tell tales of ships far out at sea.
Overwhelmed by fear and doubt,
I feel a weight, full history.

Tall tales of ships brought in from sea,
our neighbours never short of stories.
I hear the wealth of history –
this house has had its share of glories.

Our neighbours never stint on stories:
sad ghosts, lost king, a secret tunnel.
This house would like to share its glories,
it needs an outlet, human funnel.

Lost ghosts, sad king, the hidden tunnel;
so much has happened in these walls.
I am that outlet, willing funnel.
I know that time and duty calls.

So many lives lived in these walls
and all of us just passing through.
I know my duty, time past calls.
Clear now what I have to do.

All of us just passing through,
faint traces left of who we've been.
Clear now what I want to do,
the atmosphere warm, calm, serene.

Small traces left of who we've been –
initials stamped on chimney breast.
An atmosphere that heals, wipes clean.
My mind now quiet, fears at rest.

Initials carved on chimney breast.
Those people all those years ago might
have shared my quiet, now at rest,
drawn to this window every night.

Walking to Eakring Brail Wood

Spring

Sounds thicken the air and prick up your ears. Our pace quickens at full extension, your face smudged brown from rich mounds and hedgerows ripe for rummage. Eye out for fairweather neighbours with wintershy dogs, I nearly trample two locked-on frogs that make you jump. There's more goings on in Top Field – fat dozy bees stumbling around a sprinkle of yellow stars bump the Red Admiral flotilla. Nothing mars your joy, quivering like the pink ribbons on trees that mark some village rumour, but home beckons me. I dread the heat that is to come.

Summer

Scowling at the glare, I've made you wait till well past twelve but now you need to go. Just a short one. Calm, and slow. Must try to blank how much I hate these flies, the hard cracked ground, rank roasted smell of crap and tip, this itchy scratch and sweaty slip, my half-blind squint. With one bound, you crush a careless bird under the oak, won't give it up. My sudden sneeze the only breath to stir the wheat, no breeze to stroke its willing ears today. You choke and spit brown feathers in the dirt, fast panting as we scuttle into shade, ignore my ranting.

Autumn

Although this morning rattled geese flew off the field in chilly mist, at noon we pass an empty pitch of broiled earth, mass marker stalks where corn once grew, hot empty graves. I sniff in vain for telltale hints of rot, while your untroubled nose roots past crumbled dust and goes, unwelcomed, into spider's veil and rodent larder. No time to spare, up we go till harder soil confounds us and we stop. You're grateful for a gentle hand; soft, slow lickings remind me that ever-ready pup has grey-flecked ears now. So few berries left. Such slim pickings.

Winter

Worth the steaming puff to reach the top at sidestitch pace, I'm tugged up until I stop to let you off, ignore the stencil sign that says you should be kept on. Released, you rush around to sniff and pee and track, the ground too hard to dig. Lined up at my back, whiteout apple ghosts in monochrome hush, the silent tip cloaked odourless to my right. Wave after wave of furrowed blankets spill to the road, our house a small red glow to fill a gap in wood and church and hill. The sight prods my chapped, reluctant lips to praise gunmetal clouds on these goosegrey days.

Coal

The widows wrote for coal that cold, wet winter
of '53, when smog stoppered cities, the Empress
sank, waves sucked the east clean and Perry Como
kept stars from getting in their eyes. In their distress,

biros surged across cheap lined pages, curling and
looping like seagulls crying in the storms, school-drilled
copperplate working thin black seams glittered with tears.
Sweetness restocked shelves in February, but nothing filled

the displaced hearth, stoked the flue, kept their kettles
boiling. The widows chopped up chairs; tables and beds
lost their legs, wardrobes spilled lying wedding lace
onto rugs. Old wood spluttered in the grate like dead

husbands promising to return, vowing homes for life,
pledging never-ending coal to warm a miner's wife.

Three witches

Ernehale 1971

Inside this plastic barrel, on this
playground, I see all the colours
of summer spin by like the kaleidoscope
in Mrs Blatherwick's art class. They
roll me over and over and over. I know that
the marks on my legs and moles on my neck
won't be any smaller when they let me out, so
I don't make a sound. If I squeak or cry
from fear, they will tip me all the faster
and they'll win. Even though the pounding
of their fists and the hiss of 'witch, witch,
witch' makes them seem older, stronger,
harder, they are only five, just like me.

Bilsthorpe 1595

I am Joan Bettyson of Bilsthorpe, healer of
cows, gatherer of herbs, loyal daughter and
god-fearing, church-going wife, falsely
accused this day by friends and neighbours of
the Devil's work.
Shame on you – shame on you all,
who drink the milk and take your calves to
market with sleek round bellies
filled by their mothers' flowing teats.
If I were what you say – and I protest
I am not with every breath, every
paternoster ave, my knees creaked to the floor
to crawl to Jesus – if I were such a woman,
then by God you would know a reckoning that
would make the church tower tremble as it
did in the day of Gilbert de Gand,
warmonger and whoremaster of this parish.

But I am not, and the earth and sky are
quiet, and light with summer, and
the scent of rosemary fills the air.
Smell it now, my good friends, and then
release me.

Bilsthorpe 2013

When she rang the bell, I really was
up to my oxters, between six different,
pulled from pillar. So it wasn't a lie
to say I didn't have time to buy, or offer an
upturned palm for forecast of doom or
happiness, depending on her taking of me.
And she took it well, looked me down and up,
saw the day's stress in the falling hairgrips,
the mess of mud and straw on knees, the top
lip only pink stain and smeary specs.
But I was ready for her. I'd rehearsed, was
quite prepared to catch her curse and blow it
back through tunnelled fist, with a gentle
whisper to be careful who you mess with.

Notes

Part One: How to Knit a Sheep

Bert's Pig (p. 16) : 'The farm was occupied by Mr Bert Godfrey and his family for many years. You could buy a bale of straw for 6d. He had a very large boar pig there that had a fearsome reputation, hence the very thick door to keep it in.' [www.picturethepast.org.uk]

Doubtful Words (p. 18): Bert Godfrey's son Richard provided many useful research documents, several of a personal nature. One of these documents was a Post Office telegram from 1948 offering wedding congratulations to his parents - 'May your basic rations be health and happiness' - with the standard phrase 'For free repetition of doubtful words telephone "TELEGRAMS ENQUIRY" or call, with this form at office of delivery' printed at the bottom.

Critical Paths (p. 32): Livestock create different tracks and paths across the land over time. As prey animals, sheep have evolved to have 270 degree vision and goats an incredible 320 degree vision; their paths curve to enable them to see what might be following behind with lunch on its mind.

Part Two: Washing Eggs

The notes below are from *The Chicken Manual*, Haynes Publishing. For more information see www.haynes.co.uk.

Point of lay (p. 40): the stage of its life at which a chicken can start to lay eggs, usually at the age of about 16-20 weeks …

Imminent lay is heralded by their faces, combs and wattles becoming redder, and they may well start to make throaty noises often described as a sort of soft 'cawk cawk' sound.

Shedding feathers (p. 41): The female will lay most of her eggs in her first season, following this with a moult of her feathers and growth of a new set ... during this stressful process laying is suspended as the hen diverts all of her energy into replenishing her feathers ... Basically the chicken's body can't cope with regeneration and reproduction simultaneously. A good layer will drop all her feathers seemingly overnight and will recover quickly if in good health.

Hybrid (p. 42): A bird with parents from two different breeds; used today as a term for commercial laying birds ... hybrids bred for free range are typically more robust and hardier than those bred for cage production.

Predictable (p. 43): Egg colour is normally related to the colour of the chicken's ears – red ears produce brown eggs while white ears produce white eggs.

Squat (p. 44): First approach the chicken and put a hand firmly on her back while pressing down lightly; this induces a squat, as the chicken thinks she's being trodden on by a cockerel. Some hybrids are actually bred specifically to squat when you approach them, to make handling that much easier.

Clipping my wings (p. 45): Clipping one of a chicken's wings is carried out to unsteady the bird in order to prevent it from attempting to fly over a barrier ... you should only ever clip one wing – if both wings are clipped, you won't actually unsteady your chicken, only hamper it until it eventually learns how to compensate.

Blind gut (p. 46): Caecal dropping: every seventh to tenth dropping voided by a chicken comes from the caeca or blind gut; it's of a foamy consistency, easily distinguishable from a normal dropping.

Crock (p. 47): As part of their communal lifestyle, hens will try to lay in nests that already contain eggs, and will often move eggs from neighbouring nests into their own, which is a practice utilised by breeders, who put crock (china) or rubber eggs into a nest to promote laying.

Oddity (p. 48): Oddities occur in a number of forms. Probably the most common is an egg with a thicker band of shell around its middle. This is often caused by a shock, such as a loud noise or even a sudden rain storm, when the egg stops momentarily in its passage through the hen's system and extra shell is deposited …

Parasites (p. 49): Weight loss, malnutrition and depression are typical symptoms of a worm burden in general … According to ancient wisdom the best time to treat worms is when the moon is full, which is when they're supposed to be at their most active.

Gular flutter (p. 50): Gular flutter: term used to describe the fluttering of a chicken's throat that helps it to cool down … The nasal opening functions as a heat exchange system and helps to reduce water loss, aided by the chicken panting and fluttering its throat.

Egg bound (p. 51): If the egg is the wrong way round, or too large … it will become stuck and subsequent eggs will back up. The hen will stand hunched and may exhibit signs of distress as she strains to pass the egg … the best method of treatment is to keep her warm and quiet, and put a little KY jelly or liquid paraffin into the vent with your finger.... If it remains stuck due to its size, then gently pierce it and remove all the fragments (any left behind can cause further injury).

Pecking order (p. 52): Living in a large communal group termed a flock, a strict hierarchy exists to promote social harmony. There is a strict 'pecking order', with a dominant male and female having access to the best feeding and nesting areas. If this social balance is upset by removing a dominant bird or introducing another, fights will occur, sometimes resulting in serious injury, until the balance of order is restored … the highest ranking bird will peck all those beneath her, while the lowest ranking bird is pecked by all.

Grit (p. 53): While oyster shell is optional, flint grit is a necessity and should be permanently available to your birds, as it helps to grind food in the gizzard in much the same way as millstones grind grain into flour.

Broody (p. 54): Spotting a broody is easy: she looks well but refuses to come out of the nest box, if disturbed she squawks and fluffs up her feathers and either shuffles around or pecks you, and if you pick her up out of the nest box she'll sit indignantly on the floor clucking and will often defecate a large stinking mass, which isn't pleasant.

Red and green (p. 55): (Boredom) … manifests as feather pecking and vent pecking in adults and toe pecking in chicks. If blood is drawn the birds quickly become frenzied in their attacks, as they're drawn to the colour red, and cannibalism can result … hang up bunches of green stuff to provide a distraction.

Too long with ducks (p. 56): Chicks hatched with ducklings will often adopt very duck-like habits, and you'll have difficulty integrating them with other chickens.

Quota (p. 57): At birth, a female chick has a limited number of egg cells in her ovaries, and this is the maximum … that she will ever produce. The more a hen produces early on in her life, the less she will produce later.

Part Three: Bildr's thorp

Nottinghamshire Sheet XXIX N.W. (p. 61): The Ordnance Survey map of 1920 covering Bilsthorpe and surrounding villages shows several farms and other natural landmarks which either vanished or were 'repurposed' as the village moved away from its agricultural past into an industrial era. Wycar Leys is now a care home.

Bildr's thorp (p. 64): 'The choice as a defensive site was perfect, the marshy land at the base was commanded by a 60 foot rise of Keuper rocks terminating in a small plateau about 300 feet above sea level … Not until the mediaeval period were the original defences augmented, in the case of the manor house, by two moats lying west and east of the site. These still remain to protect the Manor Farm which replaced Bildr's original stockaded Thorpe.' From *Bilsthorpe – A History*, Bilsthorpe Heritage Society.

Völuspá revisited (p. 67): In the Edda, a collection of Old Norse poems, Bildr is one of the dwarves fleetingly listed in the Völuspá, the prophecy of the seeress. He is a minor character, whereas Baldr, son of Odin, is one of the major players in Norse mythology, having a whole section of the

Edda devoted to his untimely and much-lamented demise.

Vivat rex (p. 71): 'Throsby preserves a tradition that in Bilsthorpe Hall, near the church, Charles I for some time concealed himself from his enemies, and the cupboard in the manor farmhouse is still shown where he is supposed to have been secreted. Possibly the incident may have occurred when his Majesty proceeded to join the Scottish army at Newark after escaping from Oxford.' [www.nottshistory.org.uk]

Ex cineribus resurge 1726 (p. 72): 'A great part of the village was burnt down in 1726, and by a Latin inscription on Mrs Outram's house, we are informed that it was restored from the ashes of the fire by Elizabeth Broughton.' [*White's Directory of Nottinghamshire*, 1853]

Their letters (p. 74): Letters written by illicit lovers were a key piece of evidence in a Jacobean trial for adultery, Walker v. Roos, as documented in the Laxton Transcripts. While the content of the letters has not been recorded, the court transcripts reveal the drama of the affair through the sworn testimony of friends and neighbours living in Bilsthorpe. The full court transcripts are held on the University of Nottingham website: http://mssweb.nottingham.ac.uk.

Fox and cubs (p. 76): The common name for Pilosella Aurantiaca, an orange hawkweed from the daisy family which grows in drifts as a wildflower on embankments, roadsides and churchyards like St Margaret's in Bilsthorpe. The National Census of 1911 showed a farming family called Fox living in Bilsthorpe, with four family members including two young daughters, five servants and farmhands, and 14 people in total dwelling at the location. Although Manor Farm is not mentioned specifically, the Godfrey family succeeded the Fox family in taking over the tenancy of the farm when it was sold as part of dismantling the Rufford Abbey Estate in 1938. [http://discovery.nationalarchives.gov.uk]

The man who taught Milton (p. 78): 'In the ancient parish church lie the remains of several eminent men, among the foremost of whom is Bishop [William] Chappell, to whose memory there is a tablet at the west end, with a flattering Latin inscription. The prelate was born at Laxton in 1572, and after proceeding through his university course at Christ's College, Cambridge, became Provost of Trinity College, Dublin, and Dean of Cashel, being subsequently appointed Bishop of Cork and Rosse [sic]. He appears to have been a learned disputant, for in Fuller's 'Worthies' reference is made to a debate taking place at Cambridge, in which he so disposed of the arguments of Dr. Roberts, of Trinity College, that the latter had to be carried out of the theatre in a fit; and King James, who was present on the occasion, taking up the thread of Roberts' disputations, was obliged to relinquish his position, 'thanking God that Chappell was his subject and not another's, lest he should lose his throne as well as his chair.' Chappell was the author of a book on the method of preaching, and he also wrote his own biography. Flying from Ireland in consequence of the rebellion in 1640, he sought the secluded parish of Bilsthorpe, of which his friend, the Rev. Gilbert Benet, was Rector, and died in 1649 at Derby.' [www.nottshistory.org.uk]

Coal (p. 84): When miners died, their widows and family not only lost their automatic right to tenanted homes which were provided by the Stanton Company or, later on, the Coal Board, they also lost their coal allowance. The archives at Bilsthorpe Heritage Society have preserved copies of letters written by widows living in straitened circumstances, asking for coal.

Three witches (p. 85): '21 Feb. 1594-5. Joan Bettyson, of Bil-
sthorpe, widow, publicly infamed (as it is said) for witchcraft.
Being examined on oath she answered "that shee divers times
within two yeres last past when she was required to helpe cat-
tle that were forspoken [bewitched] did for their recovery use
15 pater nosters, 15 aves and three credes in honour of the fa-
ther and the son and of the holie ghoste, and that theruppon
the cattle amended, and for everie of theim she had usually a
penie, poore folkes excepted of whome she tooke nothinge,
denienge that she used in that behalfe anie other ceremonie
and was taught this by her late grandfather Robert Meakin
late of Mansfield Woodhouse deceased, and otherwise shee
saieth she cannot lawfully bee charged with anie unlawfull
practices in this behalf, neither will hereafter use this anie
more. And so enjoyned upon paine of lawe that shee hereaf-
ter do not take anie such matter upon her. Yt is thought good
to the courte that shee bee dismissed without furder exami-
nacion untill other matters shall lawfully come against her
touchinge the premisses.' [www.nottshistory.org.uk]

Acknowledgements

Some of these poems, or versions of them, have appeared elsewhere. 'Hybrid', 'Diptych' and 'Their letters' were originally published in issues 47, 51 and 58 of *The Interpreter's House* (2011, 2012, 2014) – 'Their letters' has also appeared on The Poetry School's CAMPUS blogsite and in The Emma Press *Anthology of Mildly Erotic Verse*, 2nd ed. (2016). 'Squat' was published in Poetry Lostock's 2012 poetry competition anthology. 'Pecking order' and 'Eakring Brail Spring' were published in *LeftLion* in 2011, and 'Critical paths' appeared in *Brittle Star* 36 (2015). 'Gular flutter' was included in *Magma* 59 (2014). 'Three witches' was published in *Black Balloon* (2015) and 'Reward for Winter' included in Second Light's *Fanfare* anthology (2015). A video recording of 'Rehomer's prayer' appeared online in *The Guardian* BookBlog on 8th October 2015 and is now on YouTube. 'Nottinghamshire Sheet XXIX N.W.' was commended in the 2015 McLellan Poetry Prize and won first prize in the 2015 Four Corners International Poetry Competition – 'Walking to Eakring Brail Wood' was commended in the same competition.

The refrain '…[he] found peace here when there was none for him elsewhere' in 'The man who taught Milton' is a phrase from *The King's England Nottinghamshire* by Arthur Mee (Hodder & Stoughton, 1938). The *Haynes Chicken Manual* by Laurence Beeken (Haynes Publishing, 2010) was an invaluable reference for a novice hen keeper and curious poet, that curiosity extending to *Society, Religion, and Culture in Seventeenth-Century Nottinghamshire* by Martyn Bennett (Edwin Mellen, 2005). I am very grateful to Richard Godfrey for his patience and time in providing such rich source material from his family archives, similarly for the helpful conversations and abundant information provided by all at Bilsthorpe Heritage Society.

I am also grateful for the expert advice of Mahendra Solanki and Jenny Swann, and the editorial enthusiasm of Jamie Mc-Garry. I would like to thank John Clegg, Jonathan Edwards, Helen Ivory and my fellow students at The Poetry School for their useful feedback on many of the poems which appear in this collection. Thanks also go to my aptly-named research assistant Courtney Woolhouse. And I am especially grateful to Alan Slaney for helping to make my smallholding dream a reality, when most sensible husbands would have packed their bags and petitioned for divorce.